MY GREAT GRANDPARENTS

Here's something you don't see every day... This is a photo of my Great Grandparents, James Charles and Fairest Weatherly, and their family. The boy in the center is my Grandfather, Les Weatherly. The boy on the left is my Great Uncle Houston, and the girl is my Great Aunt Mozel.

MY VERY FIRST MEMORY

Back before the age of no iron clothes, steam irons or spray starch, in order to get the wrinkles out of clothes you had to use a sprinkle bottle. It consisted of an aluminum top that had holes it in and a cork that would fit into a soda pop bottle filled with water.

I was about 3 years old and was sitting on a linoleum floor in the kitchen of the project house we lived in over by Seely McCord Elementary School in Benton Harbor, Michigan. My mom was ironing our clothes in the kitchen and talking to her friend. She picked up the sprinkle bottle that looked just like the one in this picture. The bottle slipped out of her hand and she dropped it. It hit the floor right next to me and made a large crashing sound. The bottle bounced off the floor, landed on its side and was spinning around spewing out water onto the floor. It didn't break, but it scared me enough to stay in my memory for the rest of my life.

THE OLD SWIMMING HOLE

Back when I was a little kid about 5 or 6, we lived in the "Projects" over on Shelly Drive which is now a housing community and the road has been renamed to Nate Wells Sr. Dive. It was just down the street from the Nazarene Church that we attended and the Seeley McCord Elementary School where I went to Kindergarten.

We didn't have any money, but we were still able to have fun. My brothers and I would get together with some of the other boys from the "hood" and go down to the "swimming hole" in the summer. The "swimming hole" was nothing more than a huge excavation hole that had been dug in the side of a hill by the ravine that ran along the back side of the projects.

Back then I didn't know how to swim at all so most of the time I just stood on the side and watched the other guys having fun. One day I saw an inner tube laying on the bank of the "swimming hole" so I grabbed it up and proceeded to float on the water with it. I guess the boy that had brought it didn't like that idea so he swam out to where I was and pushed me off of it so he could get on it.

It's a good thing that my older brother was close by and saw what happened because I sank like a stone! To this day, I still remember the feeling of panic that set in as I tried desperately to fight my way back to the surface and all I could see was brown, muddy water in front of me. Then, a pair of hands grabbed me by my flailing arms and lifted me up so I could breathe!

My brother Don had saved me, but he was angry! He was angry at me for taking the inner tube and floating out into the water because I didn't know how to swim, and he was angry at the other boy who had pushed me off of the inner tube without even bothering to see if I was ok!

We went back home and never did tell my parents what had happened and I never went back to the "swimming hole" again.

ST. MATTHEW'S CHURCH

This is St. Matthew's Lutheran Church on the corner of Colfax and Kline in Benton Harbor. Back when I was a kid, my brothers and I would walk all the way down Colfax to get to downtown so we could go to the Liberty or State Theater to watch a movie. I don't know why but whenever we passed this church it always gave me a sense of peace and belonging. I'm neither Catholic nor Lutheran but I guess it doesn't make any difference to God.

SUPERIOR STEEL CASTING COMPANY

When I turned 7 years old my dad got a job working for the Superior Steel Casing Company which used to be located in the spot where Harbor Shores golf course now sits. Just before you got to the road that led in front of Superior Steel, there was a set of train tracks and a Watch Tower that is no longer located there. I have seen photos of it before it was taken down and moved to wherever it is now.

This memory is not about Superior Steel or the watchtower however. It is about the new life that Superior Steel Casting Company afforded my family. With the new job my mom and dad were able to move us out of the "projects" on Shelly Drive to a much nicer neighborhood that was close to the Benton Harbor High School.

We moved out of the "Projects" to a home that used to be an apartment house. The downstairs was one apartment, and the upstairs was another apartment. But with the help of my Uncles and some of his friends, my dad was able to turn it into a single family house that he and my mom and we 5 kids called home. We loved living in our new home at 970 McAlister Ave.

We quickly made friends with the neighbor kids and I'm sure the quiet neighbors that lived next door were none too pleased to have us rowdy kids screaming and running around in the yard all the time, but they didn't complain, at least not to us.

That house gave us a sense of belonging and warmth that I had never known before. It was the first place that I actually felt "at home". Even as a little kid, growing up in the project, it never felt right. It never felt like home. Even at that young age, I knew we were destined to find a better life. We did exactly that when we moved to McAlister.

I remember the first day of school at Sterne Brunson Elementary (which apparently has now been converted into an apartment complex). I was supposed to walk home with my brother Don but when I came out he wasn't anywhere to be found. I just started walking with the other kids down May Street towards Colfax.

I couldn't remember which street I was supposed to turn on and I got scared and started crying. One of my classmates that I had met that day asked me what's wrong and I told him I couldn't remember how to get home. It turned out that he lived just on the other side of the ally that ran behind our house.

This new classmate was Jeff Weaver. I'm sure a lot of you know him. He walked with me the rest of the way home and we became good friends.

THE MICHIGAN FRUT CANNERY

The Michigan Fruit Cannery was the a factory located near downtown Benton Harbor, Michigan. It ran 24/7 and had 3 shifts. Benton Harbor had the largest open air Fruit Market in the world at that time. The land around the area was almost all farms and most of them grew some type of fruit. Apples, strawberries, cherries, blue berries, etc. Picking, packing and canning these fruits was a full-time job for most.

My mom worked the night shift there back in the late 50s before she went to work at the VM Company. The Fruit Cannery closed down in 2004 and the buildings were sold. It's behind the building where the Wolf's Marine is located now. Here is the history of the Michigan Fruit Cannery...

Dean Foods, with 119-year history in Benton Harbor, will shut down soon
Nov 7, 2004

BENTON HARBOR -- For 119 years there was a company in Benton Harbor making canned food products.

But on Friday, the end for what is now Dean Specialty Foods at 248 Ninth St. will come for approximately 40 workers. The company decided to get out of the diet and nutritional drink business, and the Benton Harbor plant was its only one making those products.

Approximately 25 office, mechanical and maintenance workers will remain until early December, said plant manager Dorothy Munao.

She said the actual total of people losing their jobs is 93, because some employees were on layoff.

The Benton Harbor business traces its origins back to 1885, when Charles H. Godfrey started a cannery under the name of C.H. Godfrey's Canning Works, according to a company history.

In 1927, what was then Godfrey Packing Co. merged with canning companies in South Haven and Fennville to form Michigan Fruit Canners Inc.

New owners of Michigan Fruit Canners came on board in 1962 and 1974.

The company's name was changed to Comstock Michigan Fruit in 1998 when Dean Foods acquired the plant.

As indicated by the 1954 News-Palladium article, the plant once canned vast amounts of fruits and vegetables grown in Southwest Michigan. The article said there were 1,700 growers supplying the Michigan Fruit Canners plant, which had about 100 full-time employees and added up to 500 more during harvest season.

Production of canned pudding was added in 1966, snack dips in 1973, cheese sauces in 1982 and diet and nutritional drinks in the 1990s.

In July 1998 the facility canned its last locally grown produce -- cherries for pie filling, according to Chris Palma, supply chain manager, who has worked there 36 years.

In March of last year, Dean Specialty Foods moved production of most cheese sauce and pudding to its plant in Dixon, Ill., putting about 50 of the Benton Harbor plant's employees out of work.

Bacon, the Dean Specialty Foods vice president, said the plant's equipment will be auctioned off during the first quarter of next year and then the facility -- the production and office building, two warehouses and the former research building -- will be put up for sale.

THE AGE OF ELECTRONICS

I can remember as a child growing up in the '50s, sitting in front of a 19' black and white Motorola counsel television. The one in the living room was always broken so I had to watch the one in my mom and dad's bedroom. They both worked jobs that forced them to leave the house early so I would go into the room, turn the TV on, and a test pattern with an American Indian would come up on the screen with a solid, steady beep emitting from the speaker.

Since I was usually the first one up (my sister and brothers would still be asleep at this time) I would turn the volume down so I wouldn't wake anyone and I would patiently wait for the screen to change, and the announcer to say 'Welcome to the start of another broadcast day. We broadcast on a frequency of (I didn't understand what they were talking about at that point so I tuned my little listening ears out) but finally he would say 'And now, our National Anthem.' At this point I would get excited because I knew that soon I would be watching cartoons.

To my young mind it was amazing that someone could broadcast a cartoon or movie or any type of picture with sound through the air and that with the use of a piece of metal on top of the roof we could grab that broadcast out of the air and bring it down to our television. I had no idea of how it worked, I just knew that it made me happy. Thus, the seeds of a future electronics consumer were sewn.

Back then, even the 8mm movie camera my mom and dad owned couldn't capture sound , only movies, and because of the cost of film and developing, that movie camera would only see the light of day on special occasions such as Christmas, Easter, graduations and funerals.

As a young child, I was not big into music. My mom and dad only played Country music (back then it was called Country and Western) in the house and my dad would take matters into his own hands if any of us kids touched his radio alarm clock to change the station. I grew up hating Country and Western music. I just knew that when I was older I would have my own radio alarm clock and it would be tuned to anything besides the Country and Western station.

I noticed as I was getting older, that things were starting to change. We went over to my Uncle's house one day and he too had a 19' black and white counsel TV (his was a Zenith and was in the living room) but there was a difference. He could actually change the channels without getting up from the sofa and turning the knob. He had what he called a 'clicker'. I stared in disbelief. I never knew something like this 'clicker' even existed. It was astounding. I asked my dad if we could get one and he said he didn't need one of those things because he had us kids. If he wanted the TV volume turned up or down or the channel changed he could tell us to do it.

The following year I was further awe struck when we took a trip to my Aunt's house down south and I found that she had an amazing box on her walls called an intercom. You could be all the way on the other side of the house and she could talk to you from the kitchen to let you know supper was ready without having one of the kids run down the hall screaming that it was 'Time to eat!'

A few years passed and I guess my dad started making better money because something wonderful happened. We got a new 25' counsel TV for the living room. I was looking for the 'clicker' and was disappointed when the delivery men didn't put it down on top of the TV. However, that disappointment soon turned into absolute overjoyed enthusiasm when the TV was finally hooked up and turned on. It was a COLOR TV! It was beautiful. The cabinet was oak and it had doors and when you lifted the lid on the right side of the cabinet, it had a built in AM/FM radio and a record player! This was too much! I was so excited I could hardly breathe. I actually had to run upstairs to the bathroom before I made a mess in the living room.

Back then, we only received 3 stations: ABC, CBS and NBC. I soon found out that most of the shows were still being broadcast in black and white, but NBC was starting to broadcast more and more programs in color. I couldn't wait for the announcer to come on to say 'This program is being brought to you in stereophonic sound and in living color', and watch the black and white peacock spread his tail feathers to turn into those glorious pink, yellow, blue and green colors. Unfortunately, on our television, most of the screen was a sickly green color, but in my young mind I thought, 'How could it get any better than this?' Life was good and before my mom and dad would get home from work, the living room would be filled with the sounds of music. Real music, like The Beatles, Herman's Hermits, Sonny and Cher, anything other than the dreaded Country and Western.

Now, things are different. A LOT different. Children today have only to push a button on their MP3 players to listen to anything they want within the privacy of their own head by the use of ear buds or Bluetooth headphones. Televisions are no longer pieces of furniture in oak cabinets to be marveled at.

Televisions today are monstrously large flat panel pieces of art that open to a world of 500 channels that are not only in color but with the advent of 1080p Hi Def, and theater like surround sound, they look and feel almost real enough to step into.

It's hard to imagine, but as fantastic as it seems to be, somewhere in the future, the technology that we and our children enjoy today will seem as old fashioned and archaic as the scenes I described from my early childhood.

Oh, BTW, I'm much, much older now and I LOVE Country Music!

MOVIE HOUSES IN THE AREA

Back in the early 1900s Benton Harbor was the place to be! It is located on the shores of Lake Michigan (one of the largest fresh water lakes in the world) and was a thriving place for tourists coming from Chicago and Detroit. It had a world famous amusement park (Silver Beach), lots of beach front property, the largest open air fruit market in the world, the House of David amusement center, and plenty of shopping and entertainment.

In doing some research about old theaters in the Benton Harbor area, I came across some interesting finds. In the early 1900s Benton Harbor actually had an OPERA HOUSE! It was the BELL Opera House and located near the Fruit Market. It seated 900 people.

Also, at one time Benton Harbor had 4 movie theaters operating. The State, The Liberty, The Lake, and The City Theaters. Coloma (another nearby town) had one movie theater, the LOMA. I've only been in it once and that was back in 1990 when "Dances With Wolves" was playing. Benton Harbor also had one of the first Drive-In Theaters in Michigan, the Starlite. Of course, the Starlite Drive-In theater is no longer around. It is now a Car Lot on M-139.

ST. VALENTINE'S DAY

Back before God was kicked out of public schools, before Political Correctness rotted everyone's minds, Valentine's Day was called Saint Valentine's Day after the 3RD century Roman Saint who was commemorated each year on February 14th. He was known as the Patron Saint of Romantic Love.

We used to give out little St. Valentine Cards like these in school. We would pass them out either before class or during recess so it would be "anonymous". Everyone would be excited to see how many they got! Of course the "popular" girls would get the most cards.

I ALWAYS made sure to put one on the desk of the "not-so popular" girl so she wouldn't feel bad. I learned that lesson in 3rd grade when that year one of the girls didn't get any cards put on her desk and she was so embarrassed she started crying and ran out of the room. From then on I promised I would never let that happen again.

THE KENNEDY ASSASSINATION

When I was growing up in Benton Harbor, it was a wonderful place to be. Back in the '50s and early '60s Benton Harbor was like living in Mayberry, USA. All the neighbors knew each other, all the kids knew every other kid for blocks around.

Back then it was no big deal to have a neighbor come over and watch the kids for a couple of hours while you ran to the post office and the bank or stopped to do some shopping at the Woolworth Store. People actually talked to each other, they trusted each other and they helped each other without even thinking about getting paid in money.

It was a quieter, peaceful life. Kids would get dressed for Sunday school in a little suit and tie or a nice, colorful dress. Hair was combed or brushed, shoes were clean and polished.

Back then, the men wore suits and usually a hat and the women wore a nice dress and makeup before ever even thinking about leaving the house.

People were just more polite back then. Men would hold the door open for a woman and the woman would say "Thank You". People would smile and greet each other on the street. Guys dressed in white shirts and khaki pants would greet you with a smile at the gas station and fill the tank, check the air in the tires and check the oil under the hood all at no extra charge.

Going to the Woolworth store or the five and dime was a treat so the kids wouldn't act out in public. They did whatever their parents told them to do or else they would get "The Look" and they knew that meant trouble when they got home.

Back then the streets of Benton Harbor were all lit up with Christmas decorations on every light pole and hanging over the streets from the traffic light wires. All the stores were lit in Christmas decorations and people were doing their Christmas shopping downtown.

But then things changed.

President Kennedy was shot and killed in Dallas Texas on Friday, November 22, 1963.

On that day, I remember sitting in my 5th grade class when a knock came on the classroom door. The teacher went over and spoke in a hushed tone to one of the ladies who worked in the office.

When the teacher turned around, she was crying! I was taken by surprise because I never in my life had seen a teacher cry. It's just one of those things that they don't do. When you're a 10 year old kid you don't think about your teachers as being actual people with feelings. You could never even imagine them even using the bathroom!

But she was crying and she announced to the class, "Children, something terrible has happened. President Kennedy has been killed." And with that, she broke down in sobs. We all look at each other like "What do we do now?" and nobody knew.

After a few minutes, she finally regained her composure and told us that school would be closed for the rest of the day and that we should get our coats and gloves and go home.

With that announcement, one of the kids in the back of the room shouted "Yay" and everyone turned around and gave him a look of "What is WRONG with you?" We got our coats and boots and gloves and all filed out in a single line.

Nobody said a word the whole time until we were outside. Some of the kids started running towards home, some of the girls were crying, and I had a sick feeling in the pit of my stomach as I slowly walked home. I don't think I even lifted my head the whole way. I just kept staring at my shoes as they crunched on the snow step after step.

My mom and dad came home about an hour later. They both had been let out of work early that day and my mom was crying. I remember her sobbing and saying "Why did they have to kill him? Why? They could have voted him out in a year! Why did they kill him?" She was inconsolable. My dad had that same look on his face that he always got when somebody was about to get a spanking. I was a little scared of what might happen.

My dad turned on the TV set and the only thing that was on every channel was news. No Garfield Goose, No Three Stooges, not even a soap opera. Just the news.

All weekend long, the TV stayed on and again, all that was on was the news. We actually watched as Oswald was shot by Jack Ruby, and we watched the funeral procession. We saw John F. Kennedy Jr. salute as the horse drawn carriage passed by. We saw Jackie Kennedy in her black veil. At that time, I wondered why the horse without a rider had boots in the stirrups that were facing backwards. I later learned that was to honor the dead.

We didn't go back to school until Tuesday the 26th of November and things had changed. You could feel it in the air. The innocence of Mayberry/Benton Harbor had died along with President Kennedy.

People weren't quite as friendly or trusting of each other after that. It's like a veil had been lifted and people were starting to open their eyes to the truth of how nasty the world can be.

After that, LBJ became President and the Viet Nam war went into full gear. Every week you could read obituaries in the New Palladium or the Herald Press about "Local boy killed in Viet Nam" and they would show a picture of a young, 18 or 19 year old boy fresh out of high school in their uniform with the details of who his parents were and his brothers and sisters and when the Florin Funeral Home would be holding services. It was depressing!

Even as a young boy I never could shake the feeling of "What's wrong with people?" I couldn't understand why things couldn't go back to the way they were just a few months before. But they didn't. They never did.

I truly believe that the assassination of JFK was the true turning point that changed life as we knew it, not just in Benton Harbor, but all over the country.

ENTERTAINING OURSELVES

I remember a lot of things that happened on my street while growing up in a much more simple time than now. We were good friends with a lot of the kids in the neighborhood. The Sears family across the street, the Lauer family across the street, the Sitensticks, John Henberger, the Browns down the street, Jeff Weaver before he moved to Union Street, Dennis Herman, and the Schaeffers who lived across the ally and two doors down.

Most of the time, my younger brother and I played with the Sears boys across the street. We would play kick the can, hide and seek, dodge ball, and a few games we even made up that didn't have names but they always involved running and trying to tag someone.

Back before video games or computers, we all had to rely on our imaginations to have fun. My younger brother and I used to wear a towel tied around our necks and pretend that we were Super Heroes fighting the "bad guys". We even had a secret identity and our "superman pills" which were those little candies called "smarties". We would eat one of those and on would go the towel "cape" and we were transformed into batman or superman or the flash!

We all knew better than to wander out of ear shot of mom and dad. When it was time to come home my dad would step out on the front porch and he'd better not have to yell more than once! Even "superheroes" can get their butts kicked by dad.
We also had other places that we found entertaining.

Sledding or tobogganing down the hill behind the Benton Harbor High School.
Ice skating at Whittlesey Park or Union Park in the winter.
Playing pool at the Campus Que

Bowling at the Blossom Lanes Bowling Alley
Going to the Star Lite Drive-In or the St. Joe Auto Theater
Seeing a movie at the State, or Liberty Theater
Roller skating with those awful metal skates that attached to the bottom of your shoe and they NEVER rolled smoothly
The Silver Beach Amusement Park
The miniature golf course in front of the Fairplain Plaza

It seems like there were endless ways to find entertainment back then that somehow no longer exists today.

THE ICE ANGEL

Winters in Southwest Michigan could be brutal, there's no denying that. Being a kid, we had to make the best of what we had. You got dressed as warmly as possible and protected yourself from the elements. You did the best you could. I actually didn't stop liking winters in Southwest Michigan until I got my driver's license. Then I hated every minute of it.

But long before I started driving, living in Michigan during the winter was wonderful.

We could go ice skating!

Every year when I was growing up, Union Park would flood their field and turn it into a wonderful, huge ice skating rink for everyone to enjoy. Entire families could be seen out on the ice have a great time. Union Park even had a "skate house " or "warming house" where you could go and store your street shoes, put on your ice skates and come back in to get warmed up when you had been outside for too long and were freezing your butt off.

Whittlesey Park had the same thing but that was all the way in St. Joe, so I always went to Union Park because I could walk there from my house.

When I was 8 or 9, I got my first pair of ice skates. They were hand me downs from my older brother, Don. They were a size too big for me so I had to wear 3 pair of socks to keep my feet from slipping inside and getting blisters. They got blisters anyway. They were hockey skates, not ice skates. The difference is, hockey skates don't have a toe stop (groves cut into the front tip of the blade) and the blades are a little thicker and longer than regular ice skates.

The first time I tried to ice skate, I was terrible! I was down on the ice far longer than I was standing on the ice! Of course, Don, my older brother was much better than me and he quickly found a girl and took off skating with her and just left me to fend for myself.

I tried and tried to move forward on the ice but all I could do was scoot along like some drunken guy who couldn't keep his balance and I kept falling on my face or my butt. After a while it didn't make any difference which.

Then, an "older woman" (she was probably 15 or 16) asked me if I was ok. I said "yeah… I'm ok, I just don't know how to work these dumb skates." She said "Here, let me help you" and with that she took my hands and she pulled me forward as she skated backwards. I was elated! I was doing it! I was actually moving forward on the ice without falling all the time! She said "See… it's not that hard. Just push out with each foot. Skate on the left foot while pushing out with the right foot, and then skate on the right foot while pushing out with the left foot. Just keep doing it that way and pretty soon you will be skating like a champ."

I fell immediately in love with her. She was so nice and so patient and she was beautiful! She had deep blue eyes, a bright smile and long blonde hair. I was convinced she had to be an angel.

After about 15 minutes of teaching me, she finally said "I have to go now. You just keep doing what I showed you and you'll be fine. The next time I see you I expect you to skate with me!" And with that she took off towards the skate house.

I never did see her again, and believe me, I looked. I came back to Union Park every single weekend to skate the rest of the winter. I never found her, but with practice I learned how to skate pretty well. By the time I was in High School I could skate backwards, do figure 8's, jump over people who fell in front of me, just about anything.

But that one act of kindness from a total stranger stayed with me for the rest of my life. To this day I still think of my Ice Angel.

BAD MEMORIES

Not all of my childhood memories were happy ones. They are just the easiest to remember and the most fun to write and read about.

I have a lot of good memories about growing up in Benton Harbor, but every once in a while some bad memories come creeping through.

I remember a time that my younger brother and I were sitting on the porch and my friend, Mike Sears came riding up on his bicycle. He was excited because there was a group of his friends all meeting at somebody's house and were going as a group to a little league baseball game being held at the field down on River View Drive. He asked me if I wanted to go but I had promised my little brother that we were going to the park to play that day.

Instead of me keeping my promise and taking my little brother to the park, I jumped on the back of Mike's bike and rode off toward the game and my little brother was calling my name begging me to come back. He started crying and I felt so bad but I didn't have the guts to tell Mike to stop and let me off. To this day it still bothers me that I did that.

Another memory involves being blamed for something that I didn't do.

For Christmas, my brother Don got a BB Gun. I know it was a Daisy but I don't know if it was the same kind as Ralphie got in the movie "A Christmas Story" and no, I didn't shoot my eye out.

Two houses down from us, the neighbors had a cage in the back yard. Actually it looked more like a chicken coop and they were raising pigeons. I had borrowed my brother's BB Gun and was walking down the alley behind our house because I was going to the High School.

In those days, there was a swamp behind Fieldstrip Field and they had a lot of Cat Tails (the plants that look like corn dogs) and if you shot them with a BB then they would explode with a million little puffs of cotton flying out. I was going to go shoot some Cat Tails.

As I passed the neighbor's chicken coop full of pigeons, I saw something that looked odd. There were two or three of the birds lying still on the ground. They were dead. I stopped and looked at them wondering what might have killed them but then I just shrugged my shoulders and walked on towards the school.

After a fun couple of hours of shooting cat tails and watching them explode, I headed back home. When I got there one of the women from the pigeon house was there talking to my dad.

Apparently she had seen me walking in the alley with the BB Gun and found the dead birds and thought I had shot them with the BB gun! She was quite upset and stormed off towards her house. My dad started yelling at me about shooting the neighbor's birds. I protested and told my dad I didn't do it but he was angry and he grabbed the BB gun and smashed it up against a tree and it bent the barrel so it couldn't be shot again.

Then he made me go down to that house and apologize to them for shooting their birds. I tried to tell the lady that I hadn't done it but she was convinced otherwise so I had to tell her I was sorry and it would never happen again. Not only had I been wrongfully accused and convicted of a crime I didn't commit, it had cost my brother Don his favorite Christmas present. I never forgot about that. I probably never will.

The last bad memory involves the first real job I ever had. I had worked picking fruit when I was 7 and had a paper route when I was 10 but this was a real job that paid real wages. I was a car-hop at the Dog ˜N Suds Restaurant that was located on Empire down the hill from the High School towards Riverview Drive.

I was 14 when I got that job and it only paid 50 cents per hour. I would work 3 nights during the week and then Saturday and Sunday. I would usually bring home about $20 per week and maybe 2 or 3 dollars in tips. Back then the usual tip was a dime and if they really liked the food and service, a quarter! It was a rare thing indeed to get more than a 25 cent tip!

Ed Radeski was our boss. He owned the franchise and he was a fair but firm man who never took any guff off his employees. If you smarted off to him or was rude to a customer you found yourself fired the next day.

I had recently obtained a Ducati motorcycle (it wasn't much more than a scooter) as it only had a 60cc engine. I loved that bike and I rode it to work on a Sunday. It was a slow work day and Ed decided he was going to take the day off. He told the head cook to watch the place and he would be back in a few hours. The head cook was just a high school kid and wasn't much more mature than the rest of us so we decided to take advantage of the "free day" we had just been given.

We started pouring ourselves free root beer drinks and eating Coney dogs and Texas twin burgers without recording them for payment. Then I came up with a brilliant idea. I was giving free rides on my motorcycle in the parking lot! After a few free rides I decided to pull an Evel Knievel so I propped the restaurant doors open on both sides and rode the motorcycle straight through the restaurant! We all thought it was pretty funny.

The next day, I was fired. It seems that instead of taking the day off, Ed had a storage shed located up on the hill behind the restaurant and was sitting up there watching everything we were doing including my "Greatest Show On Earth" tricks with the motorcycle.

It didn't really bother me that I lost the job. It bothered me HOW I lost the job. Because of my own stupid actions, I got myself fired from the first real job I ever had and I never forgot that.

THE FAMILY CAR

Back in the late '50s we moved to a house at 970 McAlister Ave. in Benton Harbor. At that time, our family car was a 1956 Blue & White Ford. We were all getting bigger and the car just couldn't hold the entire family anymore. This photo on the left was taken in 1960.

In the Spring of 1961 I came home from school and was surprised to see a Red and White Chevy Station Wagon parked out in front of the house. I was wondering who had come to visit. Then I found out that the car belonged to us! The story I was told was that my dad had won it in a game of pinochle. But the 1956 Blue & White Ford had disappeared from the driveway so I think he actually just traded it in.

The station wagon is pictured on the right. We used to have so much fun with this car. The tailgate would be let down and my brothers and I would ride down the road with our feet hanging out of the back of the car! There were no seat belt laws back then and none of us used them. It's a wonder we survived!

This was the car that I remember going to the Starlite Drive-In Theater in as a kid, and it was perfect for holding the whole family and still have room to crawl in the back and go to sleep during the long movies like "How The West Was Won".

SILVER BEACH AMUSEMENT PARK

When you're a little kid, what could be more fun than going to an amusement park? Nothing! Nothing can get you more excited, get you up out of bed and dressed in a flash than mom or dad saying "Hey, it's such a nice day out, how about if we go to Silver Beach today?"

Silver Beach Amusement Park to me, was hands down, the best part of growing up in Benton Harbor Michigan when I was a little kid. The sounds of the rides, of kids screaming and laughing, the smell of popcorn, cotton candy, and taffy wafting through the air as you walked down the midway. The bells and chimes coming from the Penny Arcade or the sound of the screams of happy and frightened kids coming from The Comet roller coaster as it descended that first steep drop.

One of my favorite rides was the bumper cars. When you're only 7 or 8 years old, getting behind the wheel of a car, no matter what it looks like or how small it is makes no difference. In your mind you are driving a real car and you have power! Power to race around the metal track with the sound and smell of electricity crackling above you as the rod that extends from the rear of the car to the ceiling sends sparks over your head. Then bam! Someone hits you from the side and sends you off in another direction. It was so much fun. No video game made today can give a kid the same type of joy that they could get from a 5 minute ride on the bumper cars.

As you continue down the midway, there were kiddie rides. Tiny boats that floated in a round moat with moms and dads taking photos of their 3 o4 year olds sitting behind the wheel of those boats. I never paid much attention to those rides because I had my mind set on one thing...

The fun house! Without a doubt, the fun house was the place to be as a little kid at Silver Beach. I would literally spend hours in there. I would have gladly set up a bed and spent the night there if I could have. There were so many things to do!

Of course the first thing you had to do was grab a small rug and head up the wooden stairs so you could slide down the huge wooden slide! Then you could sit on the flat spinning platform that would go so fast it flung you off into a padded carpet area. Some of the bigger boys were brave enough to stand in the middle of it with their legs spread wide and their arms stretched out. They looked like Leonardo Da Vinci's drawing of Vitruvian Man as they spun around and around. Afterward, they looked more like an impression of Foster Brooks stumbling around looking for another drink!

There were the wooden slats that moved back and forth and you tried to walk them without holding onto the railings but 9 times out of 10 you only made it 2 or 3 steps before falling off or clinging to the railings while your legs and feet moved back and forth, back and forth beneath you.

Then there was the rolling barrel. I believe it was call the Barrel of Fun. I loved going on that one! The purpose was actually to be able to walk the entire length of the barrel and back without falling but I didn't care. I knew that my little legs and uncoordinated body would never make it, so I made it my mission to try and climb the sides on all fours as far as I could while the barrel was turning and gravity was pulling me back down. I remember watching in amazement as one of the other boys went to the middle of the barrel, stretched out his arms and legs and was able to touch both sides and hold himself in that position while he got turned all the way upside down and then back upright again! I thought to myself, when I get big enough I'm going to do that too! Alas, it was not to be, by the time I was old enough and tall enough to do that, Silver Beach had shut down.

But the cream of the crop, the top of the bill, the ultimate ride in the Fun House was The Sugar Bowl. It was the ride that everyone waited for. It only operated a few times per hour. Usually, when I saw kids starting to line up to get on I would stop whatever I was doing and get my butt over there so I could ride too. It was so much fun. It was a huge wooden bowl shaped ride that you sat in (some people lay down) and it spun faster and faster until you were held against the sides by centrifugal force. To me, this surely had to be how the astronauts trained to prepare for space launch. I found out later that I wasn't exactly wrong. They didn't use The Sugar Bowl for training, but they did go through a similar training for Centrifugal Force.

After becoming almost exhausted of being in the Fun House for a few hours, my older brothers always wanted to go in the house of mirrors. I did not like the house of mirrors as a little kid. There was this mechanical clown sitting out there that laughed maniacally the whole time and to me it looked and sounded evil. Once you were in the house of mirrors it was like being trapped in a maze that you had to try and escape from. I have always been claustrophobic and in there the panic would set in hard. It seemed that no matter which direction I went I would wind up bumping into a glass wall. I just knew that I was never going to get out and some day some cleaning lady would stumble across my dry bones lying on the floor in the corner. But my older brother always knew when I had enough and he would come back, hold my hand and lead me out to safety.

There were other rides and amusements further down the midway, I believe a Ferris Wheel, and of course, the Shadow land Ballroom all the way at the end by the Pier, but I never paid any attention to those until I got old enough to go on dates.

Then there was the roller coaster, The Comet. It was the ultimate scary ride when I was a little kid. Nothing could possibly be any higher or faster or more frightening than The Comet at Silver Beach as far as I was concerned. Since I had never been to any other amusement parks at that stage in my life, I had no idea that it was considered rather tame compared to other roller coasters.

The feel of anticipation as you're waiting to get on, listening to the other kids and adults screaming and then those screams turning into laughter as the cars returned to the station. The butterflies in your stomach as you get on and they put the chain around your waist to hold you in the seat and you grab onto the bar to steady yourself. The clink clink clink sound that the huge chain would always make as the cars climbed higher and higher towards that first huge drop. When you arrived at the top, if you still had your eyes open (which mine usually were not) you could see all the cars in the parking lot, all the people down on the beach and Lake Michigan that seemed to go on and on forever. It was so beautiful, such a serene, moment... Then...

Terror clutched my mind as the cars dropped down that first incline. My stomach was in my throat and I just knew we were all going to die! How could something like this be legal? How does anyone survive this ride? How could my brothers do this to me? I'm only 7 or 8 years old, I'm too young to die! But instead of crashing into the ground, the cars start to climb again, then down again, then back up again higher and higher, slowing the cars down to take that first curve to the left. For a moment you think we are going to fly off the tracks into mid-air and land on top of the penny arcade. But, the cars make the turn and down they fly again. Some of the older kids are laughing and holding their arms high above their heads. I'm thinking, "NO WAY", my hands are grabbing this bar and I'm holding on for dear life!

After a few more dips and turns the cars start to head back to the station where all of the screams turn into sighs of relief and laughter and we see the next group of victims waiting eagerly to take their ride. Me, I'm just glad it's finally over. Glad I actually survived the ordeal. My brother turns to me and says "Let's do it again!" I smile a huge beaming smile and say "Yeah! Let's do it again!" and off we run to get back in line.

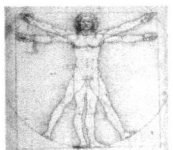

CRAZY THINGS TEENAGERS DO

When you are a teenager, you do crazy things. It's part of growing up and finding out who you really are. I have already written about how I got fired from my first two jobs because of the crazy things I did. Here are a few more.

When I was in 8th grade I was friends with a group of boys that consisted of Joe Flaugh, Bob Gifford, Kenny Webster, and Don Schaeffer . We used to hang out together on the weekends, go to the beach, play at the park and sometimes do things that would have gotten us into trouble had anyone found out.

Joe Flaugh and I were best friends back then. He lived about 3 blocks down Colfax Avenue from my house and we used to walk to the Jr. High together. One day in the spring, while walking to school, we spotted a beer truck sitting behind Golka's Grocery store and being the curious type we decided to investigate. We found that the sides of the truck were rolled up and entire cases of beer were exposed and there was not a soul in sight. Apparently, the driver was busy making a delivery inside the store and was most likely stacking the beer inside the walk-in cooler. That would be the exact same walk-in cooler that I would be crawling out of about a year later if you remember my earlier post.

We proceeded to abscond with a 6 pack of Miller High Life (we didn't think we could get away with a case) and ran all the way down the alley until we reached the back of Patton Brother's Appliance Store. There, we stashed the new ill-gotten treasure under a box in the corner. The next day, we stopped at that spot, retrieved one of the beers and shared it before we went to school. I didn't really like it at all. I only took a few sips and then I let Joe have the rest of it but we thought we were really something. We had gotten away with it! It was the "perfect crime" for a couple of inexperienced 14 year old kids.

The next day we went back to the spot, only to discover that the trash had already been picked up and all the boxes, as well as the remaining 5 cans of beer were gone. So much for our "perfect crime" spree.

Another crazy stunt that I pulled in 8th grade was during the summer vacation. That group of boys that I mentioned decided we were going to have a "sleep over". My parents had taken my younger brother and went up to Fremont Lake for the weekend and my older brother Don was always out on a date with his girlfriend so that just left me to watch the house. We all met at the park at 9:00 am and spent the day riding our bicycles around town. We rode down past the High School and on to Riverview Drive. We stopped and threw stones into the St. Joe River before proceeding to ride our bikes across the Blossomland Bridge into St. Joe and down to Silver Beach. After spending the day at Silver Beach we rode back to my house and watched TV until about 11:00 pm.

We decided that 11:00 pm was too early to just go to sleep but there wasn't anything really good on TV so we needed something else to pass the time. That's when Don Schaeffer announced "bicycle races!" It was a pleasant, warm summer night so we thought it would be cool to have our bicycle races up and down McAlister Avenue with nothing on but our underwear. We were screaming and whistling, and generally making a nuisance of ourselves. I'm sure the neighbors were probably lying in bed thinking "Oh my God, it's those crazy Foster Boys again. What in the world are they up to now?"

Apparently, one of the neighbors didn't have a sense of humor and they called the police because we heard a siren coming down Empire Avenue and heading our way. We quickly dumped the bikes in my back yard and snuck into the house through the back door. The cop car turned off his siren, slowed down, and was shining his spot light at all the yards as he passed my house but by then we were already inside. Another "perfect crime".

But the craziest thing that I did that summer was to dye my hair. I've always had dark brown hair. I took after by grandfather on my dad's side of the family. He always had dark brown hair even into his '70s.

I remember this particular day that my buddy, Bob Gifford and I were listening to the new Beatles Album "Sargent Pepper's Lonely Hearts Club Band". For some unknown reason, we decided that we were going to dye our hair blonde. No, I don't know why we decided to do that, but we did. He and I counted up the money we had between us and found that it was just enough to get a box of Miss Clairol Ash Blonde Hair Dye from the store. Bob also had dark brown hair and it was longer than mine. Back then I wasn't allowed to have long hair like all the "hoodlums" as my mother called them.

We read the instructions on how to prepare the mixture, put on the gloves, and proceeded to dye each other's hair. We waited the correct amount of time that the instructions said and then washed out the dye. We were both shocked to see that instead of having Ash Blonde hair, we both had orange hair. ORANGE HAIR! We looked like Bozo the Clown without the clown makeup! I was devastated! I just knew my life was over! I was sure that when my mom and dad saw what I had done I would be grounded for life! I jumped on my bike and rode home to see if I could do something about this clown hair before my mom and dad got home from work. My brother Don was home when I got there and when he saw my hair he burst out laughing. He literally fell on the floor because he was laughing so hard. He knew that my fate had been sealed.

I ran upstairs, locked myself in the bathroom, took off my shirt and proceeded to wash my hair as vigorously as possible with a bar of ivory soap. I must have washed my hair 6 times before they got home. But each time I looked in the mirror…. ORANGE HAIR! I even tried putting shoe polish on it but all that accomplished was a brown stain on the back of my neck and it ruined my t-shirt.

When my mom got home and saw what I had done she grabbed me by my arm and shoved me in the car. She drove me over to Golka's Grocery and parked in the parking lot and practically dragged me across the street to Bass Barber Shop.

When Heigie Bass (pronounced HI-GEE) saw my mom he said "Hi Mrs. Foster, what can I do for you today?" She was so mad that she could barely get the words out so she pointed to my hair and hissed between her teeth "Cut it off! Cut it ALL OFF!" "I don't want a single hair left on his head!"

Heigie was doing everything in his power not to laugh out loud. I heard him choking back a laugh when he saw the brown stain running down the back of my neck. I sat in the chair and never said a word the whole time he was taking the electric clippers to my head. He never asked me what happened, he never asked me why. He just concentrated on making my head look like a polished apple while my mom sat in the chair across from me and watched. If you have ever seen a cartoon character that was so angry that steam was shooting out of its ears, you would have a good idea of what my mom looked like while sitting in that chair.

Back then, haircuts were only 75 cents and when he was done giving me a buzz cut, my mom tried to give him a dollar for the service but he just shook his head and said "No charge today Mrs. Foster, you have a nice day." I do believe he was just as scared of her as I was.

I was grounded, but to my surprise, not for the rest of my life. Not even for the rest of the summer vacation. I wasn't allowed out of the house for 2 weeks and the next time I saw Bob Gifford, his hair was just as short as mine.

SUMMER VACATIONS

When you are a little kid, nothing can come close to the excitement of Summer Vacation except perhaps school holidays!

New Year's Eve was a night for the adults at my house. My sister would babysit us while my mom and dad would go out for the evening. Usually, they would go to the Moose Club or sometimes to the Joker's Club for a night of rowdy fun. We didn't have the big ball drop to watch on TV but I remember they always had a show with a "Big Band" playing "Auld Lang Syne" on the TV. It might have been the Mitch Miller Show. The next day we always got to go out and build snow forts and snowmen in the yard. Sometimes for dessert, we would make "Snow Cream" which is Ice Cream made out of fresh snow. In the days before "Acid Rain", my dad would always scoop a huge bowl of snow up and then mix in some vanilla extract, some milk, and some sugar to make snow cream. You had to eat it quickly or it would turn into a mushy liquid but it was really good.

Valentine's Day (which was actually called St. Valentine's Day when I was a kid) was nice. You got to make up little valentine cards and either put them in a box for the teacher to pass out or you placed them in an envelope on the desk of those special people that you liked. Then you anxiously waited to see if you had any coming back your way. Sometimes they would include a little candy heart with words like "I Love You" or "Be My Valentine" and the girls would whisper and giggle as they watched you open your envelope.

President's Day (Originally we had two holidays for this – George Washington's Birthday and Lincoln's Birthday which were combined along with JFK's Birthday to become President's Day). We actually got out of school for that day and usually the day before they would have a school assembly in the gym where the younger classes would hold a skit that included George Washington cutting down a cherry tree and saying "I cannot tell a lie father, I chopped down the cherry tree" and Abraham Lincoln would say "Four Score and Seven Years ago, our fathers brought forth upon this continent a new nation dedicated to the proposition and all men are created equal." A little later they added John Kennedy saying "And so my fellow Americans, ask not what your country can do for you, ask what you can do for your country."

St. Patrick's Day, everyone had to wear something green to school and sometimes the teachers would hand out sugar cookies in the shape of shamrocks with green icing and green kool-aid to drink before the end of the day and everyone got a napkin that said "Happy St. Patrick's Day" to catch all the crumbs from the cookies.

April Fool's Day. Although not an official holiday, it was one in the mind of a child. Kids trying to play jokes with other kids or on the teachers was usually a lot of fun. Sometimes, not so much. Sometimes kids went too far by placing thumb tacks in chairs and watching the reaction of another kid sitting on them. The kids who did it thought it hilarious but the one who sat on it didn't think so at all. One girl who sat on a tack screamed and jumped up so hard that she banged her knee on the bottom of her desk and had to go to the hospital for x-rays.

Easter was usually part of Spring Break so everyone looked forward to that. As a kid, we boys would always get dressed in our suits and tie and my sister would put on a frilly dress and a ribbon in her hair and we would all go to Church on Easter Sunday. Back then we attended the Free Methodist Church which we would walk to because it was only about 6 blocks from our house on McAlister.

After church, we would come back home and find our Easter Baskets filled with candy and colored eggs. The baskets were made of handcrafted wicker and were brightly colored with pink, blue, green and yellow colors. There would be chocolate bunnies wrapped in tin foil, jelly beans, circus peanuts (the orange marshmallow kind), hard boiled eggs that we had spent all afternoon the day before helping to dye blue or pink or yellow or green. Sometimes we would have little gifts like crayons and coloring books or whistles or yo-yos all resting on top of green strands of nylon that was supposed to look like grass.

Then we would all pile into the car and take a drive out in the country towards Berrien Springs down US-31.

We would pass all the usual sights in M-139. The Comet Store, Mike Young's, the Roxie Brown Lantern on the left side, down a little further and the Kroger on the right and the McDonalds on the left. The Fairplain Plaza with the Miniature Golf Course, followed by Henry's Hamburgers on the left and Louie's Tavern on the right. Angelo's Party Store and Goldblatt's are on the left and the Gas Station in front of the Shopper's Fair on the right. Now we come upon the Star Lite Drive-In Theater. A little further on the left is Blossom Lane's Bowling Alley followed by Howard Johnson's. On the right is the Red Roof Inn and just on top of the hill behind it is Bill Knapp's Restaurant. Now we pass under the I-94 overpass and on the right is the Holiday Inn.

Next, we cross over the bridge that spans over the St. Joe River and we head into Scottsdale. There's the Mark III Restaurant on the left and on the corner is the church with the small cemetery behind it. Another mile and we are really out in the country. Hardly any buildings anywhere out here. Just small farmhouses and lots of farmland.

There on the right are some small red signs, one after another spaced about 1/10 of a mile apart. "He lit" "A Match" "To Check" "His Tank" "Now They" "Call Him" "Skinless Frank" "Burma Shave". Another mile and we spot the old barn on the right-hand side of the road with the painting of the Kreamo Bread advertisement on the front. Then a little further on the left there would be the DX gas station and we knew it was time to turn right onto Rocky Weed Road. Another quarter of a mile on the right was my grandparents' house located about 300 yards back from the road.

We always went to my grandparents' house on Easter so we could meet with the rest of the family. Aunts, Uncles, cousins from both sides of the family would gather here for a lunch and the annual Easter Egg hunt. My grandparents lived on a farm with a huge front yard and a backyard that extended out to a forest. There were hundreds of places to hide Easter eggs and I'm sure that we never found all of them.

After the Easter Egg hunt, we would all sit down to a big lunch. Then it was time to make Ice Cream! We got out the old wooden Ice Cream maker, my grandmother would put all the ingredients together and all of us kids would take turns cranking the handle to help make the best Vanilla Ice cream ever invented.

Memorial Day. We always had a long weekend and would take a trip up to Muskegon, Michigan and spend the weekend at Fremont Lake. We would rent a cabin on the side of the lake and would spend the entire weekend swimming, boating, and fishing. The lake was huge and filled with speckled bass and sometimes if you hit a school of them you would pull in fish as fast as you could throw out your hook. I have home movies of my Uncles and grandparents holding up stringers with hundreds of fish on them that we had caught. I learned how to gut and clean a lot of fish as a kid. We would put as many as we could in the freezer and had many, many meals of fish. Whatever we couldn't fit my dad would give away to his friends at Superior Steel.

Next was Summer Vacation! That long, 3 month holiday that every kid who goes to school looks forward to every year. Back then we would get out after the 1st week of June and didn't go back until the 1st week of September so it really was 3 months of no school. We would play outside until dark, go over to the park and play catch, or in the public pool, slides, monkey bars, swing sets, or board games in the game pavilion.

We would build forts and haunted houses in the backyard with the boxes we took from Patton Brother's trash. We would go out on Sundays for lunch at my grandparent's house or have backyard pick nicks at my other grandparent's house on Sweet Street just off of Britain Avenue near Benton Heights.

My Aunt and Uncle and cousins from Mooresville Indiana would come up to visit and spend the weekend and we always had a great time. Summer vacation is like magic when you're a kid. You could ride your bike downtown and meet your friends at the A&W Root Beer Stand or go see a movie at the State or Liberty Theater. You could also go to one of the local beaches like Silver Beach, Tiscornia Beach, Lion's Beach, Rocky Gap or Jean Klock Park.

4th of July was always a treat! We lived close to the Benton Harbor High School and would always walk over there to watch the beautiful fireworks display. I still remember the sounds of the crowds when they would explode and light up the sky. The "oohs and ahhs" the people would make when high above them the dark night sky suddenly bursts into bright red, or orange, blue or yellow colors. How some would duck and cover their ears when a "bomb" would explode with that deafening loud "BOOM" that you could hear for blocks.

Before you knew it, September rolled back around and it was time to put away thoughts of the beach and picknicks. It was time to get ready to go back to school. A lot of kids didn't like school. I did. I always looked forward to going back. I enjoyed being able to see all the friends that I hadn't seen since last year and to meet new friends that had moved into town over the Summer. But first, we had to have school clothes.

Since I had two older brothers I usually got hand-me-down clothes from them, and most of the time they didn't fit. My brother Don was about 4 inches taller than me back then so his pants were always too long and I had to roll them up. His shirt sleeves were a little too long so I would just keep pushing them up on my arm to keep them out of my way. But every year, my mom would take me and my younger brother, John, to Woolworths on Main Street. We would get to pick out one new shirt, one pair of pants and a pair of gym shoes. I always picked out a shirt with a button-down collar and black pants. Back then they had a dress code and you couldn't wear blue jeans and Tee-Shirts to school. For gym shoes, I got Red Ball Jets because you were supposed to be able to "run faster and jump higher" with them. I remember one year my mom was complaining because they had raised the price from $2.00 per pair to $3.00 per pair for the gym shoes.

Labor Day. We always got off school for that day and it was usually starting to get cold outside so we couldn't have any picknicks or go fishing. We would usually go out to my grandparent's house in the country and my dad would help them do stuff on the farm to get ready for the coming winter months. We kids would play games and eat dinner with the cousins.

Finally, it was here… It was the 2nd most important holiday of the entire year. It was the 2nd most anticipated holiday that every kid under the age of 15 always looked forward to… HALLOWEEN!!!

I loved Halloween! We could dress up as anything we wanted, we could wear our costumes to school, we never did any real school work that day, it was a PARTY DAY! None of the kids would sit at their regular desk and all of us would be dressed up as ghosts, or witches, or Superman, Batman, Casper the friendly ghost, Richie Rich, and Archie etc.

I remember when I was in 3rd or 4th grade, we didn't have money for a real costume so my sister put me in one of her dresses and she put makeup on me and a scarf to cover my hair. I was so embarrassed to be seen at school that I went in and sat down hung my head and pulled the scarf down enough to hide my eyes so I didn't have to see anyone looking at me.

The teacher had everyone guess who the other kids were behind those masks and ghost costumes but nobody could guess who I was. I think it was the teacher (through the power of elimination) that finally guessed who I was. As soon as she did I ran out of the room, straight to the bathroom and started wiping off that stupid makeup!

That night, when it was time for Trick or Treat, I went as a hobo with the scarf tied on a stick I carried on my shoulder. We would absolutely rake in the candy on Halloween. I would go with my brother Don and my younger brother John and we would hit every house in our neighborhood and well beyond our neighborhood. We would trick or treat for hours!

Back then you didn't have people sick enough to put razors in the apples, or hot sauce in the candy. You didn't have a curfew of 8:00 and your parents didn't have to escort you to each house. Back then you ran from one house to the other, up one side of the street and down the other and when you got finished, you hauled in a butt load of candy!

We would take pillowcases as our candy bags and they would be half full. Sometimes, my brother, Don would have to carry John's because he was too little to carry it by himself. We would have enough candy to last an entire year! My mom always made us all dump our haul together in a big pile and then sort through it for our favorites. Mine was always Snickers bars and I would grab 2 or 3 of them right away. We were allowed to eat up to 3 bars that night and then the rest of the candy got put away in the kitchen cabinet to be handed out as needed (but we always climbed up and helped ourselves anyway).

The next big Holiday was Thanksgiving. Thanksgiving was a special family time. This time, instead of everyone meeting out at my grandparents in the country, everyone would come to our house on McAlister. My Uncle Jack Weatherly and his family, both sets of grandparents, my brothers and sister, sometimes my cousins from Mooresville, Indiana would come up and my Uncle Jim and Uncle Chuck would usually stop by.

We had one of the smallest kitchens in the world! There was hardly enough room to turn around in that place but somehow, my mom and my grandmothers always found a way to cook enough food to feed this entire army of people in the house.

We always gathered around the dining room table, bowed our heads as my Grandfather (Grand Dad) said the blessing and then everyone would start passing around the mashed potatoes, gravy, turkey (I always like the dark meat) the southern dressing, yams, green beans, chicken and dumplings, 3 bean casserole, and just about anything else you could possibly want. We always had a huge punch bowl full of my mom's famous fruit salad and pecan, apple, mincemeat or pumpkin pie for dessert. Afterwards, everyone would go into the living room and sit in front of the tv set or a game of some sort such as Monopoly would ensue.

By the end of the year, we finally came to the ultimate, top of the line, Grand Prize Winning holiday of all holidays, Christmas!

We always loved Christmas. Not just because of the gifts, but because it was just a magical time of year. Everyone in the neighborhood just seemed a little bit friendlier at Christmas time back then. You could hear kids singing Christmas carols at the Fairplain Plaza, store clerks would smile and wish you a "Merry Christmas" as you picked up your bags and headed toward the door.

The streets were decorated all over downtown and at the plaza. Houses were decorated with bright red, blue, green, yellow and white Christmas bulbs around the windows and doors. You could see Christmas Trees in every front room window. Christmas music was playing on every car radio and in every store.

About 2 weeks before Christmas we would all pile in the car and go with my dad to pick out a Christmas Tree. We couldn't get one that was more than 7 feet tall because our ceilings were only 8 foot and we had to have enough room for a stand and for the little angel to sit on top of the tree.

Since we had waited so long to get one, most of the really good ones had already been snatched up a week or two before. After several "Oh, I like that one only to find out that one had half its side missing or the bottom branches were already dead, we would finally all settle on "the best one".

My dad would pay the man the $5 for the tree and he would tie it to the top of the car and off we would go. We would bring it into the front room, put it in the tree stand and then turn it around until we had the "best side" pointing out.

On would go the Christmas lights. Not the tiny, blinking lights that trees have now, but the teardrop lights that came on a green wire and if one went out, they all went out. Usually, we would spend an hour replacing each bulb until we found the culprit. Next, we would always put on the bubble lights and had to make sure that they were standing upright so the bubbles would be going toward the ceiling. I always liked the bubble lights best.

Then we would put on the ornaments. Little plastic Santa Claus ornaments, fragile bulb ornaments, candy cane ornaments, snowmen ornaments. Next was the garland. Long, strands of aluminum or plastic garland that came in an assortment of colors.

Finally, came all of us kids' favorite decoration, the tinsel. Long, thin strips of aluminum that looked like chrome. We would always start out placing them very carefully on the lower branches so they looked like icicles but by the time we got to the taller branches, we just kind of threw them at the tree and hoped they caught on the needles to stay put. The tree would be proudly displayed in the front room window so the neighbors who passed by could enjoy our work of art too.

On Christmas Eve, my family would once again all gather at my grandparent's farm in the country. All of my cousins, aunts and uncles, my immediate family, and grandparents from both sides would be there. We would pile all the gifts all the families had all brought under my grandparent's huge Christmas tree and after eating our usual meal would start passing out the gifts to everyone.

Most families pass out gifts in an orderly fashion so everyone could see what everyone else got. Not my family. It was a free for all of tearing open packages. There was Christmas wrap and ribbons everywhere on the floor, on the walls, down the hallway, in the kitchen. If Christmas wrapping paper were blood it would look like Custer's Last Stand had occurred at my grandparents' house.

Most of the kids would squeal with delight as they tore open their gifts and would run to the giver with shouts of "Thank you, Thank you; it's just what I wanted!" Every once in a while you would hear a kid crying because his brother or sister had gotten what he "really wanted" and he got a pair of pajamas or socks.

That evening, all the families would help clean up the mess and then would go back to their homes to retire for the evening. We would go back to our house on McAlister and my dad would turn on the Christmas lights on the tree. Before long, the bubble lights would start bubbling and the little angel at the top would be lit to watch over us all. All of us kids were sent to bed and would eagerly wait to see what Santa had brought us in the morning.

SNOW DAYS

When I was in 7th – 9th grade I went to the Benton Harbor Jr. High School. Unfortunately, it no longer exists. It's been torn down and replaced with yet another housing project.

Back in those days we didn't get too many "Snow Days" like they do now. We lived on McAlister Ave and the BHJHS was located almost a mile (8/10th of a mile to be exact) away.

Now, that would seem a daunting task for today's kids to try and trudge through foot high snow but we didn't know any better and we did it every winter, 5 days a week!

Back then, about the only time the schools would close would be if the heating system (boiler) broke down.

I remember one particular winter morning getting pulled out of bed at 5:30 am by my older brother who said "Get dressed! We have to help dad get out of the driveway!" With that, I put on my pants, a t-shirt, a shirt, a jacket, my boots, my gloves and a woolen hat and waded out into the snow. My brother handed me a coal shovel and we proceeded to dig my dad's 1959 Chevy (lime green with tail fins for miles) out of a snow drift that reached all the way up to my brother's window on the 2nd story of our house! This snow was insane! It wouldn't stop falling!

I was sweating, my oldest brother was pushing the car and my dad sounded like the dad on the movie "A Christmas Story!"

After about an hour of digging and pushing and cussing, we finally got it out and he and my mom were on their way to Superior Steel Casting Company and V-M Corporation.

We rushed back inside and turned on the radio with fingers crossed, hoping that they would announce school closings and that Benton Harbor would be top of the list. Surely they couldn't expect us to walk to school in this! It was a blizzard! You couldn't see 2 feet in front of your face! There were drifts that were taller than my oldest brother!

Soon the school closings started. "Coloma Schools are closed. Eau Claire Schools are closed. Lakeshore Schools are closed. St. Joe Schools are closed...." We thought, here it comes, and our hearts sank as we heard "Benton Harbor School System is still open!" WHAT? HOW CAN THIS BE??? Every other school in the world is closed except Benton Harbor? What kind of jacked up crap is this?

But, we sullenly ate our breakfast got ready for the day and listened to the radio one last time, hoping and praying that they changed their minds but no.... we had to go to school.

My brother and I trudged onward through the snow, fighting the drifts and even walking in the streets that were half way plowed until we finally made it to the Jr. High. We got halfway down the hall and was stopped by one of the teachers. She said "What are you doing here?" "The school is closed today." "The janitor said that the boiler was out and can't be fixed until tomorrow". We just stood there dumbfounded and shivering and the teacher said "Go... Go home. No school today."

So we went back into the snow storm and fought our way back home but we never were more happy to do it than that day!

Oh.. BTW now you know why I live in South Florida!

REALLY BAD DECISION

Golka's Grocery store was a small, mom & pop neighborhood store located on the corner of Empire and Broadway. It had a total of 4 aisles that were barely wide enough to allow the small grocery carts through and if two people were trying to shop in the same aisle it was a show to see which cart would have to back up to allow the other one through.

It was a clean but dimly lit grocery store that stocked all the necessities of Milk, bread, flour, condiments, eggs, beer, wine, cigarettes, and other items that most small stores stock.

At the front of the store just to the right of the entrance/exit door they had a large gumball machine. For the cost of one nickel, you could try your luck at getting a "lucky gumball".

The lucky gumball was yellow and had two brown stripes going around each side. Most of the time you would get just a regular gumball which was not a bad deal because the gumballs were a pretty hefty size for a nickel. They were about twice the size of a regular penny gumball back in those days.

If you did get a lucky gumball, you turned it in to the cashier and she gave you a quarter! With that much money you could go next door to Olds Dairy and pig out on a large malt or go down to Bizer's Drug Store and buy 2 comic books and some candy!

Needless to say, I and my younger brother were always trying for that lucky gumball. We even had a "system" worked out that consisted of a small prayer before turning the handle.

We would recite "Please God, Please God, Let me get a lucky gumball" and would turn the handle just slightly with each word and by the time the prayer was done the handle would be turned all the way around and we would open the metal door to discover what it delivered.

After I got fired from my first job at Dog 'N Suds, I was hired as a bagboy and stock boy at Golka's Grocery Store.

After reading some of the responses from previous post, I now believe that every boy who lived in my neighborhood worked at Golka's Grocery Store at some point in their young life.

I was 15, but this was a couple of years before they started requiring kids to be at least 16 to work.

I really enjoyed working at Golka's. It was a friendly atmosphere, the owner was a nice, older, Christian woman and as long as you gave her back the magic marker you used to price the stock, she wasn't always riding your back like most of the older folks did back then.

The work wasn't that difficult. When you weren't busy bagging and carrying out groceries, you had to mark the stock and put it on the shelf. If you didn't have anything else to do, then you had to dust the shelves and sweep the floors. Simple work that anyone could do and it paid 65 cents an hour compared to the 50 cents an hour I made at Dog 'N Suds.

The two guys in the back of the store ran the meat counter. They were always cracking jokes, smoking cigarettes and occasionally making lewd comments about the women who came into the store (but they did that quietly so the women wouldn't hear them).

One evening, Mrs. Golka had taken the night off. It was a quiet evening and not too many people were shopping. I had already marked up and shelved all of the stock that had been set out for that day and had dusted and swept the entire store twice.

Remember the old adage "Idle hands are the Devils Playthings"? Well, in this case it was true.

I was bored. I had all my work done and still had 2 hours to go on my shift. Nobody was shopping so I wasn't needed as a bagboy. I decided to go in the back room and start cleaning out the cooler. The cooler was a large walk in refrigerator that had extra slabs of meat, produce, beer and wine.

I started moving the produce boxes around so I could sweep when I found a half bottle of Boone's Farm Apple Wine hidden in the corner. Apparently one of the other stock boys had either placed it there or else one of the guys from the meat counter. I didn't care. It was open, I was bored and suddenly I was thirsty.

I had never had a drink before other than the occasional sip of beer my dad or one of my uncles would slip to me at a Christmas party. This was a treasure to behold to my 15 year old mind.

I proceeded to drink the entire half bottle of wine, which I actually found to be delicious. It tasted like those little hard apple candies you could get at Bizer's candy counter. After consuming the contents of that bottle I was feeling pretty good. I also decided to try a beer. A real beer, not just a sip from my dad's open and usually warm bottle of Stroh's.

I opened a can of Budweiser and drank the whole can. Then I opened another one drank that whole can. By this time, all reasoning had left the station on the last train from my mind and I opened yet another can and drank that one too.

Needless to say, I was drunk. Not just drunk, blind drunk. I couldn't walk, I couldn't talk, I could barely crawl. As luck would have it, the Bag Boy Buzzer started buzzing. Buzz… Buzz… Buzz…

The rest of the story up to the point that I woke up was told to me by one of the other bag boys about a week later, because I have absolutely no memory of it myself.

I do remember the bag boy buzzer ringing just above the door to the back room. Apparently I didn't come forward. The buzzer went off again. Again, I didn't come forward. The buzzer went off a third time and the cashier started calling my name loudly. "Karry! Karry! I need you to come up and bag this lady's groceries and carry them out to the car!" At that point I was crawling through the backroom door past the meat counter trying to make it to the cash register area.

One of the meat counter guys looked at me and said "Oh, my God!" and started laughing and the other one said "Man, you are soooooo fired!!!!"

After that I must have passed out. One of the meat counter guys went up to the office and called my house to have someone come and pick me up. My mom showed up about 10 minutes later still in her pajamas and house coat and a pair of house shoes. Her hair was in rollers and she had on a scarf and a look that would turn any mortal man into stone if he stared into her eyes.

She grabbed me, picked me up with one hand and shoved me toward the front door. She opened the car door with one hand while holding me up with the other and then threw me into the front seat like a bag of potatoes and sped off towards home.

I don't know how I got into bed, I don't know how long I was asleep, but the next day (and the day after) I was sick as a dog! I thought I was going to die. My head hurt so badly that I thought it would explode. My stomach was doing flip flops at even the thought of eating anything. I was throwing up water and crackers!

Of course I was fired! I was fired so much that I wasn't even allowed to come back into the store to pick up my final paycheck (by the time they deducted the cost of the beer and wine – yes, they charged me for the whole bottle even though I only had half) I think I wound up with about $5.00 left.

So that was 2 jobs in a row that I got fired from for doing stupid stuff. But that 2nd one taught me a lesson that I never forgot.

Don't ever mix beer and wine on the same night.

I'm just kidding.

The real lesson was that I never did anything ever again that would put my job in jeopardy. That was the last time I have been fired from a job, but on the bright side, I actually became somewhat of a celebrity among the other bag boys at Golka's Grocery Store.

THE STARLITE DRIVE-IN THEATER

Back in the '50s and '60s it was a rare treat for us to go to the movies. My mom and dad both worked long hours to try and keep a roof over our heads and food on the table for a family of 7 people. But every now and then, if a John Wayne movie was playing, my dad would load us all into the station wagon and take us to the Starlite Drive-In Theater or the St. Joe Auto Theater!

He would always make a big pot of popcorn on the stove and put it into a brown paper bag before we left and would usually stop at the 4 winds restaurant and pick up a bag full of hamburgers and greasy French fries for us to eat because the concession stand always charged too much for their food.

If you didn't get there early, you would have to go up and down the rows to try and find a good parking spot and sometimes when you found it there was NO SPEAKER on the pole (which would explain why that good spot was empty).

After finding the best spot left available, we always ran up to the front and played on the swings, monkey bars, slide, and rode the train at the Starlite. We would always play up there until the 6 or 7 Woody Woodpecker, Chilly Willy, Droopy, or Popeye cartoons would finish playing on the screen. Then it was time to come back to the car.

You could always smell popcorn and cigarette smoke (or that terrible smell of the PIC bug repellent coil) coming from the cars and there was always a line out the door for women waiting to use the bathroom.

At intermission I still remember the music and the commercials about hot dogs, hamburgers, popcorn and "cold refreshing drinks" on sale now at the concession stand and how you should come and get it before the next feature film begins.

Somebody would always cross in front of the projection booth on their way to the men's room and would have to stick their hand up so it showed on the screen and either wave or make shadow figures or make other gestures.

At the Starlite we would always play a game called "WAHOO" It was actually BINGO played on little puch out cards that they gave the driver when paying at the front booth to get in. If you got 5 across or up and down etc. you had to beep your horn to announce "WAHOO" and come up to the projection booth for confirmation of the win. I never knew what the prize was because we never won.

If the film broke or the sound stopped, EVERYONE would start honking their horns as if the projectionist wasn't already aware of the problem or somehow that would help fix it.

About 3/4 of the way through the 2nd movie a crackle would always come across the speaker hanging on the window and the guy would say "Ladies and Gentlemen, the Concession Stand will close for the evening in 15 minutes. Thank You."

The movies were terrible by today's standards and the sound system was the worst but I wouldn't trade that experience for anything in the world! If you ever get a chance to take your kids to a drive-in movie theater, do it. It will be an experience they will remember for the rest of their lives.

The last movie I ever saw at the Drive In was "The Good, The Bad, and The Ugly" starring Clint Eastwood. It was part of a triple feature of spaghetti westerns they were playing that weekend before I left for boot camp in 1972. I fell asleep about halfway through the 2nd feature (A Fistful Of Dollars) and I didn't wake up until my dad was knocking on the car window at about 4:00 in the morning. He got worried when I didn't come home by 3:00 and came out looking for me.

THE FIRST CONGREGATIONAL CHURCH

This is the First Congregational Church on the corners of Pipestone, Belleview and Broadway. Right behind it used to be the Benton Harbor Jr. High School which has been torn down and turned into a housing project.

My good buddy Nick Tenerelli and I used to perform as a musical duo on the weekends. We would give 1/2 hour sets at different functions such as school activities, church luncheons, craft fairs, etc. He and I did a set at this church back in 1970.

It has a statue in front of the church. The little triangle of grass is called Roosevelt Park and the statue is of President Teddy Roosevelt.

DRIVER'S EDUCATION

When you are 16 there is only one thing on your mind… Well, ok, 2 things but the one that's most important is getting your driver's license! Once you got that, the other thing would naturally follow.

Back in the '60s they still taught Driver's Education classes in High School. You would sit in a classroom and one of the teachers or coaches who needed extra income would teach the class. In my case it was the football coach/math teacher who taught Driver's Ed.

You would watch movies on how to properly change lanes, how to parallel park, when it was safe to pass, what all of the traffic signs were and you would always get at least one movie of what happens if you drink and drive or don't wear a seat belt. It would be a lot of photos of actual car crashes and cars wrapped around trees, people covered in blood stained sheets because they didn't survive the crash etc. I guess that was the '60s version of "Scared Straight", Driver's Ed style.

I wanted my driver's license so badly I couldn't wait to take Driver's Ed. If I remember correctly, it was taught during Summer Vacation and it lasted about 6 weeks for the course. We would sit in the classroom and listen to lectures or watch the movies and then take a quiz on what we learned. Then….

PARKING LOT TRAINING!!!

We actually got to get behind the wheel of a real car and learn how to drive! At first, it was just in the parking lot of the school. We had to drive between orange traffic cones and not knock them over. Then we had to learn how to parallel park between orange traffic cones and not knock them over. Then we had to learn how to come to an emergency stop without knocking over the orange traffic cones. Once we mastered these techniques…

ROAD TRAINING!!!

Oh My God! We got to actually drive a real car out on the road! With other cars on the road! How cool is that? First, the teacher would show us how to properly get ourselves set for the drive. Sit up straight in the seat, put on your seat belt and make sure it's snug but not too tight. Adjust the rear view mirror so you had an unobstructed view of the road behind you. Adjust both outside rear view mirrors so you could see anything coming up on you from either side. NO RADIO ALLOWED! Put both hands on the wheel at the 10 O'clock and 2 O'clock positions. Then put your foot on the brake and start the engine. Check your rear view mirrors, turn on your blinker and slowly ease out onto the roadway.

There were usually 2 or 3 kids in the back seat waiting for their turn and they were so excited I thought they would pee their pants. The teacher was always having to tell them to be quiet so they didn't distract the student behind the wheel.

I remember the first time I had to take the wheel and go out on I-94. I was as nervous as a Chihuahua trying to pass a peach pit. My job was to drive from the I-94 exit close to Bill Knapp's all the way to the Bridgeman exit and then another student would drive us back.

As luck would have it, the highway was busy that day. In fact, it looked like a semi-truck convention on that stretch of the highway. Can you imagine being 16 years old, first time on the highway and almost every other vehicle on the road doing 70 miles an hour is a tractor trailer truck? I thought my hands were going to either break from gripping the steering wheel so tight that my knuckles were white or else slip off from the sweat on my palms!

Somehow I made it there without incident and the teacher was pleased. I think his butt was working button holes into the seat too. On the way back was a breeze! Hardly a single car on the road the whole way! I think the truck convention was all heading towards Chicago.

After 6 weeks of this I graduated! I got my Driver's Permit. I was legally able to drive with someone over the age of 21. Unfortunately for me, that meant my mother or my father and they were usually too tired from working to mess with me practicing my driving.

My brother Don was only 18, my brother Larry was already in the Navy and serving in Vietnam. My sister was in college at Anderson University in Indiana.

The only time I got to practice was on the weekends when my mom wasn't working. So I always tried to pack an entire week's worth of driving into a two day period. I would drive us everywhere she needed to go. The grocery store, the beauty salon, to visit her sister, downtown, anywhere and everywhere. I would also practice parallel parking. I got really good at that. I could actually get in and out of a space that you didn't think would be possible in a car that size.

Then the big day came…

THE DRIVER'S TEST!

I went down to the DMV which was actually on Niles Road in St. Joseph back in those days. I took the book test and got every question correct except one. It had something to do with how much space you needed to have in front of you before you turned on your turn signal.

Once I passed the written test, I had to do the road test with an inspector checking off little boxes and writing little nasty notes on a form held on his little clip board.

I was as pleasant and cheerful as I could be but inside I was dying! I was scared to death that this guy with his crooked teeth and bald head and his little clipboard and checking his little boxes and writing his little nasty comments on his little form was going to flunk me and I would NEVER get my driver's license!

The thought was unbearable! I would be stuck forever having to drive with my mother on the weekends while all my friends were out partying and at the drive-in theater doing God knows what without me! I just knew that if I failed to get my license my girlfriend would dump me and run off with BUBBA the football ape because at least HE had a driver's license and me being a loser with no license would be driving my mom to the beauty salon on Friday nights!

I went through all the formalities of sitting up straight, adjusting the mirrors, clicking the seat belt etc. etc. etc. And finally he said "Ok, pull out onto the road." We pulled out onto Niles Avenue and headed towards downtown St. Joe. He said, "Make a right hand turn at the light" so I turned on the blinker, checked the mirrors and turned onto Napier Avenue right across from the Whittlesey Park.

I thought he was going to have me drive past Memorial Hospital and across the bridge into Benton Harbor but about two blocks down he had me make another right hand turn onto one of the side streets. I made the turn and there were two cars parked up ahead on the right. He said "Usually, we do the parallel parking test in the parking lot of the DMV but since we're here, how about you park in between those cars."

I parked like a champ! Didn't need to pull back out and try again and again, I got it right the very first try! He even got out and eyeballed the distance from the curb and got back in and checked another box on his little form.

He said "Ok, let's head back to the DMV" and he gave me instructions on how to get there. I pulled into the parking lot and he looked at me with his crooked teeth and his bald head and said. "You're nervous aren't you?" I sighed and said "Yes, I really want to pass this and get my license." "My mom said I could take the car to the football game tonight if I pass." He smiled and said "Don't worry, you'll get to take the car, you did great!" "Now, take this form inside, give it to the woman behind the desk and get your photo taken for your driver's license, congratulations!"

I was thrilled! I was so excited. This meant FREEDOM!!! Freedom to drive anywhere. Freedom to drive everywhere. Freedom to take my girlfriend out on a real date without my mom or dad dropping us off or picking us up! There was only one problem. I didn't have a car. I had to borrow my mom's Chevy Chevelle with the column shift and the bad clutch that stuck all the time. But I didn't care. That was truly one of the happiest days of my life!

About a year later, after I graduated, I bought my very first car. It was a 1962 Chevy Impala. It was white with red interior. Bench seats, an automatic transmission and a V8 Engine. I bought it from my best friend, Nick Tenerelli's neighbor. It had been sitting in his garage for a few years and was in perfect condition. He sold it to me for $200.00.

I had to take out a loan from the bank and pay it back at $15.00 per month.

When I left for boot camp in 1972, I sold that car to a guy at LMC for $200.00 cash. I would kill to have that car sitting in my garage right now. I loved that car more than any other vehicle I have ever owned.

SENIOR SKP DAY

When I was a senior at Benton Harbor High School we had our annual "Senior Skip Day" and a group of us got together and went to Warren Dunes State Park.

A lot of the kids stayed down by the parking lot so they could talk and smoke, but the rest of us climbed the largest sand dune around and sat and talked or would proceed to run/roll down it before climbing back up and doing it again.

I sat in the sand near the top of the dune, looking out at Lake Michigan wondering what the future had in store for me. It was close to the end of the school year and I was about to graduate in June. I still didn't know what I wanted to do with my life. Up until that point, my whole life had consisted of my family, my friends, and my life of growing up in the Twin Cities area.

I really didn't know much about the outside world and the thought of leaving my cocoon was a little frightening and exciting at the same time. I was sitting next to people that were in my class, people that I had gone to school with for years and yet I didn't really know them. I didn't know what they wanted to be when they "grew up". I had no idea what their hopes, dreams and plans were for the rest of their lives and they didn't know mine. How could they... I didn't even know mine. All I knew was I wanted to go see more of the world and what it had to offer.

One of my buddies came up, slapped me on the back and said "Hey, this is supposed to be a fun day! Don't just sit there like a bump on a log, let's have some fun!" With that, we proceeded to run down this giant dune. I fell about halfway down the slope and proceeded to roll head over heels for about 20-25 feet before regaining my balance and running down the rest of the way. I went to the parking lot and lit up a cigarette to have a smoke. When I brought the lighter up to light the cigarette that's when I noticed that my class ring was not on my finger.

I had just gotten that class ring about a month earlier and it was my pride and joy. It was one of the first things that I designed and purchased without any input or financial help from my mom and dad. I was heart sick. I knew that it must have slipped off my finger when I was rolling down the sand dune and it was lost under that pile of sand. I ran back up to the spot where I first fell and started digging into the sand to try and find the ring. I dug into that sand all the way back down to the bottom of that dune but I knew it was gone forever. I felt like crying but there was no way I was going to do that in front of my friends.

I remembered the day that I got the catalog near the end of my junior year. How I combed through the different ring styles, the choices of stones, the inscription we could put on the inside, the emblem we could have on top of the ring. I had picked out exactly what I wanted. It was gold, with a black onyx stone, with the crest of Benton Harbor High School on top of the stone. It had my initials, K F on either side of the stone and the numbers 1971 above my initials on either side of the stone. On the inside my name was engraved.

It was perfect for me and it represented all the years I had spent in school. It represented that I was going to graduate in the top 10% of my class. It represented my life that I had spent for those 18 years living in the Twin Cities area and it represented my hopes for a bright future that lay just ahead after graduation.

I had designed it and paid for the ring. It cost $85.00 back in 1971 which is equivalent to approximately $525 today. For a kid who was only making $1.60 per hour working as a stock boy at Rizzo's Discount Grocery in Benton Heights, that was a fortune. It took me all summer, fall and winter to save up that much money. But now, the ring was gone and with it a part of my hope for the future.

About 3 weeks later, just a few days before graduation, my choir teacher, Mr. Anderson, said that I was wanted at the Principal's Office. Immediately, I thought "Oh crap, what did I do?" A million things raced through my mind. Was someone in my family hurt? Did they find out that I had gotten a ticket for speeding? What had I done to be called into the Principal's Office?

Mr. Overly was sitting in his office as Vice Principal. He saw me as I walked through the door and he motioned me to come in. He sat behind his desk and told me to have a seat. I sat down and he looked at me with a stern face. I was really starting to get worried now. I had known Mr. Overley since Jr. High School and he and I had always had a friendly relationship. I must have really done something bad for him to look like this.

He said "Are you missing something?" I was taken aback by this question because I had no idea what he was talking about. Then he said "Did you go to Warren Dunes a few weeks ago on Senior Skip Day?" I was embarrassed and I looked down at the floor. He said "Did you?" I nodded my head. I thought for sure I was going to get suspended just a few days from graduation. He said "Karry, look at me." I lifted my head and he had a big smile on his face. He held his hand out and in his palm was my class ring. I was so shocked I practically fell off the chair.

"How?" was all I could manage out of my mouth. Mr. Overly said, "Here's your ring, and this letter will explain how." Still smiling he said "Senior Skip Day is nothing new. We did it when I was going here to High School too." "Take your ring, and go back to class. Oh, and you should probably write a thank you letter to the lady that found your ring."

He handed me the ring and an envelope addressed to "Principal's Office, Benton Harbor High School, Benton Harbor, MI 49022" The letter was from a woman who lived in Chicago Illinois who had found the ring in the sand dune when she and her family had gone over there for a weekend visit. She knew that it was probably important to whoever had lost it and she was sending it back to the school so that the rightful owner could claim it.

That act of kindness and thoughtfulness was more than I had expected. She could have easily kept the ring and sold it or pawned it and I never would have known the difference. But she chose to return it to me because she knew it was important. I wrote her a two page letter telling her what had happened and a little about my life in Benton Harbor. I made sure she knew how much I appreciated her act of kindness.

I now knew there was hope for the future. I knew that there were truly good people out there in that big world. I decided to try and return that goodness by helping others as much as I could.

About a year later, I left for the US Navy. During my time on active duty, I did get to see parts of the world that I never would have gotten to see. I experienced things that I never would have experienced. But I never forgot to try and help others whenever possible.

About 17 years later I wound up selling my class ring to a gold dealer who gave me $300 for it. I used the money to help pay for medicine for my daughter who had to have open heart surgery when she was 2 months old.

I don't have the ring anymore, but at least it helped someone else to have a better future. I have the kind act of a stranger from Chicago to thank for it.

MY NEIGHBORHOOD

After we moved to the house on McAlister Ave, we became familiar with the surrounding area. 5 houses down from us at the corner of McAlister and Empire was Patton Brothers Appliances. They were the ones that sold us the wonderful Color TV console that I spoke of in a previous post.

Unfortunately, that TV was sitting in the back of their repair shop longer than it was sitting in our living room. It was constantly blowing its tubes out. Remember those vacuum tubes that used to be in all TV sets and radios before the Transistor was invented? Yep, those were the ones that kept blowing.

But other than being so close to the Benton Harbor High School, and enjoying the Marching Band as they practiced marching up and down Empire Streets and Colfax, we discovered that we had our own little community. There was an entire shopping strip mall right there at the corner of Empire and Broadway!

We had Golka's Grocery, Olds Dairy, Empire Hardware and Bizer's Drug Store! Not only that, but across the street we had Bass Barber Shop, Brown's Shoe Repair and I believe there was a dry cleaners or laundry there too. We had it made!

Everything we could want right there within walking distance of our house and our parents had no problem sending us to the store to pick up milk, bread, eggs, and even a pack of Winston Cigarettes for my dad. The cashier never even questioned it.

Patton Brothers provided us kids with endless amounts of entertainment by throwing their huge packing boxes in the trash behind the building. Those became forts and castles and haunted houses in our back yard.

Golka's grocery had everything you could want as a convenient mom and pop shopping mart. They had the wooden floors that squeaked, they had the tiny shopping carts that always had one wheel that wouldn't turn, they had one register and they had a meat counter for chops, chicken, beef and bologna! But their prices were reasonable and we always picked up the TV guide for 10 cents at the register before we left.

Olds Dairy was a fun place! It was an old time soda fountain place that served root beer floats, ice cream cones and malts! I loved that store!

Empire Hardware was dark and a little scary when I was a kid. They had wonderful toys though. Jacks, pickup sticks, barrel of monkeys, paddle ball and yo-yos! The guys behind the counter always kept an eye on us like we were going to steal something and it always made me uncomfortable to be in there.

Bizer's Drugs was the absolute most fun store! The people were always friendly and happy and they had COMIC BOOKS! I used to go there and spend hours just browsing through the comic books and reading them. Nobody ever tried to make me buy the books or hurry me out of the store. If I remember correctly I think they also had a soda fountain counter but I could be mistaken.

The Bookmobile would always come and sit outside of Bizer's Drugs on Broadway. When I was in Jr. High we used to love to go to the bookmobile and check out books. They would show up every other week and we could return the book we had and pick out another one.

Right down the street from Bizer's was Broadway Park. That place holds too many memories to count! The public swimming pool, the Game Pavilion that let you check out board games like checkers, Lincoln Logs, Chinese checkers, Sorry, backgammon etc.

The game pavilion had 4 or 5 picnic tables you could sit at and play the games. There was a baseball diamond where the basketball courts are located today. Over in the corner there was a metal slide, a jungle gym, teeter-totters and a small merry-go-round.

In the spring we would come over and fly kites in the park. Sometimes we would climb up the sides of the cement Entrance ways and sit on the top, dangling our feet. Something I'm sure no parent would ever allow these days even though the cement entrance ways are still there!

Made in the USA
Monee, IL
02 July 2020